Eternal Peace Within
A Souls Journey
My Life My Love My Poetry

A Collection of Poems By Sharon Johnston

This book of poetry is dedicated to every person who has crossed my path in this Lifetime.
Every person and experience plays an important role in my journey and the road in which I have traveled. I would not be the woman I am today without each of you touching my life.
This collection of poems is my creative expressions of life and submissions.

I am sharing my journey through this thing called life and all the experiences that have molded me into the woman I am today. My submissions are bits and pieces of the world and other people's lives as seen through my eyes. My journey is shared in the words of my poetry with each life experience that becomes more profound to me as I realize the Eternal Peace that I seek resides within.

Table Of Contents

I. My Life

A Souls Journey...10
The Love She Gave Me...13
Journal Entry I..14
Father..16
Me Myself and I..18
My Prayer...20
Journal Entry II..22
The Secrets that I keep...24
Gemini Love...26
The Price of Love..28
Journal Entry III...30
Love's Hangover...32
Love of Simple Things..34

II. My Love

He Came...40
His Vibe...42
Blackman..44
Journal Entry IV...46
Soul Mates...48
Thankful..50
Thoughts of You..52
Journal Entry V..54
Positive Life Positive Love...56

Without You..58
Silent Love..60
Journal Entry VI..62
Friday Night Blues...64
He is this thing called Love................................66
He Is Necessary..68
Contract for Love...70

III. My Poetry

The Dream...76
Captured..78
Kiss Your Mind..80
Journal Entry VII...82
Wanting and Needing...84
Let Him Go...86
Where did the love go?.......................................88
Journal Entry VIII..90
Remembering a King...92
Is My Black Still Cool?..94
World of Silent Pain..96
Journal Entry IX..98
Positive and Negative Love.............................100
I Cry...102
Journal Entry X..104
Your Smile..106
I See Perfection...107

Poetry

"Bits and Pieces of our Life as we live it
Blended together by our Creative Energy and
Captured by our Words"

Sharon Johnston

My Life

"Letting Go of the Past....
Gives you the Freedom and Courage to hold on to the Future"

Sharon Johnston

Life

"The road that we travel each and every day…..
Leaving Bits and Pieces of our Dreams and Memories
Along the Way"

Sharon Johnston

A Souls Journey

June 2, 1964 my life began
Cradled in my mother's arms
Feeling the comfort and security of my father's hand

Five years later as I laugh and play
My siblings surround me
All I remember are the happy days

Daddy's Girl I loved him so
I remember crying and throwing tantrums
Every time he would have to go

Years later I am now 10 years old
My body is changing so fast
Endless possibilities begin to unfold

A few years later
My first Love walks through the door
Innocence lost
A Virgin no more

Now I'm in my early teens
Life is so complicated
No one knows how you feel
Or what you mean

Young adult who is excited about life
New Beginnings and New Love
Who wants to make me his wife?

Seeing the world for the very first time
A husband and a family
A Love that was so Devine

Seven years later and I'm single once more
The world seems so different
Endless opportunities are knocking on my door

The days turn to months and months to years
So much Joy and Happiness
But sometimes there were tears

A Soul's Journey is the story of My Life
The Girl who became a Woman with Courage, Wisdom, and
Passion
To always do what felt right

Embracing my True beauty
And loving the Skin that I'm in
Strong and Confident My Soul's Journey
Was finding the Eternal Peace that Lives Within

The Love She Gave Me

Eyes Full of Joy that Nurtured My Pain
Peace and Comfort each and Every Time She would Call My Name
These are the Gifts of Love that she gave me

Arms that Held and sheltered me through the Years
Strength and Courage each Time She Wiped My Tears
These are the Gifts of Love She Gave Me

A Heart Full of Love and Compassion for all Things in Life
Lessons of Pain and the Struggles that come with being a Wife
These are the Gifts of Love She Gave Me

Wisdom and Knowledge to Know that True Beauty Lies Within
Pride and Dignity to Love My Beautiful Black Skin
These are the Gifts of Love She Gave Me

Passion and Desire to Always Dream
Never to Forget the Struggles of Our Past and What it means
These are the Gifts of Love She Gave Me

Ode to My Mother...."Happy Mother's Day"

Journal Entry I
August 1974

Everybody keeps congratulating me on becoming a woman. If This is supposed to be a celebration, why do I feel so bad? Not Really understanding this thing call Puberty.

I am **Beauty**, I am **Life**
I am **Love**, I am **Devine**
I am a **Black Woman**

Sharon Johnston

Father

He is the man you call
Husband, Brother, Lover, Uncle, Friend, and Son
He is the hands that held
You when your life begun

He is the mind that feeds
You the knowledge of Life
He is the man that loved you
Enough to make you his wife

He is the one who endures
The pain each time you fall
He is the one you turn to when
There is no one else to call

He is strength that holds
The family together
He is the man that
We all call Father

Dedicated to the love of my Life
My father

Me Myself and I

Me, the person I have grown to love
Myself, the one I turn to when I need
To feel love
I am the only person that will always
Be there for me

I am the strength that holds
My world together

I am the light that helps me
See in this world of darkness

I am the captain of this vessel
That carries me through this journey
Called life

I am the seeker of knowledge
That will feed my soul

I am the wisdom gained from
All my life experiences

I hold the power to change and alter
Everything that is my destiny

Me. Myself, and I
All that I will ever need
To be Complete

My Prayer

I prayed today
My silent prayer
Turned into a cry for help

I prayed for the strength
To walk away

I prayed for you to
Live another day

I Love you still

"Having Faith means Nothing if you don't Believe"

Sharon Johnston

Journal Entry II
September 1976

"Lord I love him...Please help him" Why is she praying for him and he just almost beat her to death. Lord Please help my sister find her way. Love is not supposed to hurt.

The Secrets that I keep

Always seen but
But seldom shown
A beauty so deep
There is so much more that is unknown
There are Secrets
That I Keep

There is a Mask
That's worn to hide
The pain and sadness
That will always reside
There is so much more to me than you see
There are Secrets
That I Keep

When I look into the mirror
Sometimes I see
A vision of Strength
But there is also a weakness that haunts me
From the Secrets
That I keep

Gemini Love

Gemini Love is one of a Kind
With and open Heart
And a Conscious Mind

Her Love of Life and need to Care
Makes you feel her Presence
Even when she is not there
Her Passion, Desire, and need to Please
Leaves you Hopeless, Lost
And on your Knees

Gemini Love is one of a Kind
With an open Heart
And a Conscious Mind

Her Beauty and Intelligence
Are always seen
Dual Personality that gives
You Everything You Want and Need
She wears a Suit by Day
And Stilettos by Night
Fulfilling all your Fantasies
And giving them Sight

Gemini Love is one of a Kind
With an open Heart
And a Conscious Mind

She gives you Strength and Lifts you up
When you're Feeling Low
She brings Peace to your Soul
More than you will ever Know
To Love a Gemini Women
Means Never Letting Go....

"To Know Me is to Love Me"
To Love Me is to know me"

The Price of Love

The Price of Love has no real value,
It's measured by time, distance, and travel...

The time you give and never get back,
It's going the distance on a one lane track...

The price of love can be more or less,
It's measured by life's failures and success...

The price of love has the power to heal,
Some might even say the power of real love,
Has the power to kill...

The price of love is sometimes disguised,
Leaving you empty, hopeless and causing your demise...

The price of love is what price,
You're willing to pay...

The true price of love,
You can't afford to give it away...

Journal Entry III
October 1986

I was not prepared to hear the news that my husband gave me tonight. I am still numb from hearing the words. "Your brother Joe was killed"
I never thought that the day I left would be the last day I hug my brother and tell that I love him. I Thank God I did.

"Love... Peace.... Faith... Strength...
Courage...Nourishing and Kind
Words that are Spoken but also Define.
There is so much Beauty in a Black Woman's Mind."

Sharon Johnston

Love's Hangover

His voice echoes in my heart and mind
Remembering all the good and bad times
How we use to fight all day
And make love all night
Missing him while he's away
Needing to make things right
Long conversations about life as we lay
Hanging on to every word
Never forgetting anything he would say
Wanting to believe in him
Even his lies
Won't ever forget
The day he said…It over Good bye

"A Man Admits his Mistakes and ask for Forgiveness..... A Boy hides his mistakes and looks for someone else to Blame."

Sharon Johnston

Live of Simple Things

Family gathered as we share a meal
Mommy's hands comforting me
Her words that heal

Daddy's presence even when he's not near
Watching over me from above
I have no Fears

Sister's love as she stands by my side
Always open to sharing
Nothing to hide

Reading a good book for the very first time
Listening to Music
As I enjoy a Glass of Wine

A Cool Breeze on a hot summer's day
Hearing the laughter and joy of
Children as they run and play

Simple pleasures and the joy they bring
My Love of Life is
The Love of Simple Things

"A Ray of Sun on my Face
Giving him Praise and Feeling his Grace.... There is a Tranquil
Peace that fills the Air
And there is Love and Laughter Everywhere
Loving Life and the Simple Things"

Sharon Johnston

My Love

"He Eases My Mind and Takes Control
The Very Peace That Resides Within My Soul
He is.... This Thing Called Love"

Sharon Johnston

Love

"People define and Express Love in many different ways. To say the words for most people is damn near impossible.
Love to me is like Breathing
To not show love or express it
Is Like Suffocating"

Sharon Johnston

He Came

He came into my life Unexpected
Finding that place in my Heart
That I have always protected

He came into my life bringing
Trust, Understanding, Compassion, Courage, and Love
Gifts No doubt that were sent
From a Above

He came into my life seeking a woman
Who was Passionate, Confident, Sensitive, and Kind
Wanting to make me His
As much as I wanted to make him Mine

He came into my life
For reasons I have yet to know
Tonight... He came Inside of Me
And I will never Let Him Go

"To New Love"
Ode to Rufus

His Vibe

One phone call
Hearing his voice
Started it all
I was Feeling his Vibe

Open dialogue about life
Sharing thoughts and memories Of Ex husbands and wife's
I was still Feeling his Vibe

The door opens and his energy fills the room
Wanting him to Cumm inside
No...Not yet ... This is too soon
I was Feeling his Vibe

Longer conversations about life as we lay
Contemplating....Wanting him to stay
Mental stimulation goes a very long way
I was Feeling his Vibe

When I speak my voice penetrates his soul
My Strength, Courage, and Dignity begins to show
Him all the things that were missing from his life
That he needed to know
I am really Feeling his Vibe

We are two spirits meeting for the very first time
Our Souls have collided
All I want to do...Is make him mine
Baby...I need you...Please come Inside
I will always Feel His Vibe

Hoping you feel mine

" Blackman"

I have loved you from the moment our eyes met,
My Intelligent" Black Man…

The day our souls from past to present did connect,
My "Soulful" Black Man…

My Fathers Soul has joined with your mother's soul
To make us one,

Please open your heart so this can be done,
My "Caring" and "Sensitive" Black Man…

Everything that he was you can be,
My "powerful" Black Man…

Everything she was I am, If only you could see,
My "Loving" Black Man…

I am yours through this journey we call life,
And long after the day you make me your wife,
My "Strong" Black Man…

We are connected in Spirit, Mind, Body, and Soul,
I will always love you, long after we grow old,
My "Spiritual" Black Man…

Journal Entry IV
April 1989

Lord I know you would never give me more than I can bear. But how can I go on without a part of me? How will I survive without My Daddy?

"Finding Peace in the Midst of a Storm
Is knowing that It is Found Within."

Sharon Johnston

" Soul Mates"

We speak words, without uttering a sound
We are Soul Mates

We hold each other up, without the use of our arms
We are Soul Mates

We ignite a fire in each other heart, without a single match
We are Soul Mates

We are together, even when we are apart
We are Soul Mates

We share a Spiritual bond, that exist from our past
We are Soul Mates

We are everything to each other,
That the other will ever need

We are and forever will be
Soul Mates…

Thankful

I said a Silent Prayer Today
I Thanked the Man above for Sending You My Way

I'm Thankful for your Strength and how you have Sheltered Me from the Rain
I'm Thankful for the Happiness, Sorrow, and Pain

I'm Thankful for all the Passion, Courage and Love that you gave
I'm Thankful for the Joy and all the Tears that you have Saved

I'm Thankful for the Love's lost that made way for You
I'm Thankful for Our Love and the fact that it is Still New

I'm Thankful for the long Nights of Silence and the Passion we have shared
I'm thankful and Blessed that you even took the time to Care

I'm Thankful for the Peace, Serenity, and the Woman that I Am

I'm Thankful for all my Blessings
But most of all
I'm Thankful for My Man

"Giving Thanks for a Good Man"

Thought of You

Alarm Clock Rings
And I roll out of bed
Thoughts of you
Instantly fill my head

Standing in the shower
The water runs of my face
I feel your lips touch mine
Thoughts of you
You're strong Embrace

As I slip my Dress
Over my head
I see visions of you
And your sweet caress
Thoughts of you
Gently laying me on the bed

Out the door and my day begins
Stuck in traffic
I begin to daydream
Thoughts of you
Deep inside my subtle screams

My day passes slowly
Barely conscious of the time
Thoughts of you
The day passion took control
And you became mine

The phone rings "how was your day?"
Hearing his voice I feel so alive
Thoughts of you all day
Can't wait for you to arrive

Thoughts of you once more
He's here….
Baby Come Inside

Journal Entry V
January 1996

Today my Faith was shattered. I Love my husband, I love God. All I want is a Baby. All my life I have been told that "A Child is a Blessing from God." I want My Blessing…I want a Baby.
Why is my doctor telling I can't have one?

"Betrayal comes like a Thief in the Night. It takes Your Soul and leaves you Hollow"

Sharon Johnston

Positive Life.....Positive Love

Door opens and his energy fill the room,
He was everything she ever wanted in a man and more.
Positive Life **Wanting** a Positive Love

She speaks and her voice penetrates his soul,
She was everything he ever needed in a woman and more.
Positive Life **Needing** a Positive Love

His Courage, Passion, Faith and Love,
Made her feel what was deep within his soul.
Positive Life **Feeling** Positive Love

Her Strength, Compassion, and desire to Love,
Made him desire her even more
Positive Life **Desiring** a Positive Love

Their Courage, Passion, Faith, and Love in each other,
Will keep his Positive Life connected to her Positive Love
Forever
Positive Life **Living With** a Positive Love

Ode to Larry B
"I love you beyond these words"
Sharon

Without You

I dreamt of you today
As my mind traveled back in time
Remembering the long conversations about life, as we lay
You're Erotic Kisses that taste like Wine

Falling asleep in your Arms, Waking up to make Love
Never Conscious of the Time
Kissing your left Nipple as I pinch the Right
Finding Pleasure in your Moans
And you simply holding me Tight

I feel your nature against my chest
As it begins to Rise
Fighting back all sensation of exploding
Wanting and needing to feel you inside

Inside My Love.....My Heart....My Soul
A Place where only You and God Reside
Me without you....Only for awhile
I Miss You

"To Passion and Love that last a Lifetime"

Silent Love

Silent Love please let me Hear
The Songs of your Past that
Haunts and Holds you in Fear

Living and Loving through the pain of your Past
With Words never spoken
Never wanting or expecting Love to Last

Silent Love so many Hearts you have broken
For those who have seen and never heard
Silent Love Please Speak Words

Silent Love I want to see
The Love in your Heart
That is only for me

As I Lay with You and Taste You
Touch You
Feel You
Kiss You
Hold You and Love You

My Silent Love..... No Words are needed
Love Me in Silence Forever!

"To Silent Love's everywhere"

"Love has the Power to make you Rich....And Everyone who Surrounds You will Share the Wealth"

Sharon Johnston

Journal Entry VI
October 1998

Today was filled with Love and Joy as I watched Ragine experience the Baltimore Aquarium for the first time. I can still hear her little voice saying " God Mommy we're having a Good Day" Little did she know that it was more than a good day, It was one of the best days of my life. She is my " Little Pookie" and I love her so much.

"Always Express Your Creative Energy and know that Anything is Possible when you Create it in your Mind."

Sharon Johnston

Friday Night Blues

It's Friday night
And I'm missing you
Baby I Got
The Friday night blues

Head on my lap
And hands on my thighs
Catching a glimpse
Of your nature rise

It's Friday night
And I'm missing you
Baby I got
The Friday night blues

Remote in my hand
How I wish it was my man
Wanting to kiss it softly
While I gently hold
As I watch "Love Jones"
My legs slowly unfold

It's Friday Night
And I'm missing you
Baby I got
The Friday Night Blues

Watching the clock
As time goes by
Breathing you in
Baby your taking me on a natural high

It's Friday Night
And I'm missing you
Baby I got
The Friday Night Blues

As I close my eyes
And begin to sleep
My dreams are filled with passion
You kissing, caressing, and tasting me

It's Friday Night
And I'm missing you
Baby I got
The Friday Night Blues

Missing you….Missing you

He is this thing called Love

He Eases My Mind and Takes Control
The Very Peace That Resides Within My Soul
He is....This Thing Called Love

A Presence that's Felt Even When He's Not Near
The Strength and Courage I Need To Erase All My Fears
He is....This Thing Called Love

The Smile on My Face When I Hear His Name
The Joy in My Life That Will Always Remain
He is....This Thing Called Love

The Warmth of a Fire on a Cold Winters Day
The Sound of Three Words That He Never Forgets To Say
He is....This Thing Called Love

The Quiet Serenity that is Present after Every Storm
The Contentment that's found only when I'm in His Arms
He is....This Thing Called Love

The Greatest Passion I have ever known
The Flame that Flickers within that never leaves me Alone
He is....This Thing Called Love

"Life is Eternal.... Love is Immortal"

Sharon Johnston

He Is Necessary

Like Water and the air I breathe
And all the things I hold dear to me
His Love multiplied by three
He Is Necessary

Like the moon and Stars and Sun and Rain
A soft kiss on my forehead that simply eases the pain
His love constant and true that keeps me Sane
He Is Necessary

Like the warmth needed on a cold winter day
The three words that you never get tired of hearing him say
Being reminded that you're never too old to play
He Is Necessary

Like watching a sunset over a peaceful sea
Being told there is no other place he'd rather be
The feeling I get when he's deep inside of me
He Is Necessary

Like getting a treat that you can have over and over again
Finding comfort and security in his arms
That helps you mend
Getting that ring that represents
No beginning or end
He Is Necessary
For Me

"Passion fuels you with Energy that last a Lifetime"

Sharon Johnston

Contract For Love

Words Exchanged on a Computer Screen
Hoping and Wishing he knows Exactly what I Mean
When I say that He is a Gift From Above
He say No.... This Is a Contract For Love
All the Things You need, Want, and Desire
Are Found with Me If I Am Hired

My Poetry

Poetry

"Bits and pieces of our life as we live it
Blended together by our Creative Energy and Captured by our Words"

"The Power of Peace can Free your Soul"

Sharon Johnston

The Dream

My day started with thoughts of you
Visions of your tongue gliding over my body
Doing all the things that only you can do

Please don't stop touching me there
Making me feel you, want you and need you
So totally unaware

That my thoughts of you deep inside me and my subtle screams
The wetness that I feel, Simple pleasures
Of your Kiss and Touch
Was Only a Dream

Captured

Words exchanged on a computer screen
Hope and wishing
He knows exactly what I mean

When I say I like how we converse
Exchanging words and thoughts
So on key nothing rehearsed

Photos shared new and old
One look into his eyes
I have fallen prey
This man has captured my soul

Kiss Your Mind

Can I Touch Your World
And Share Your Space
Kiss Your Mind, Your Inner Soul
Then Disappear without a Trace

Only to Return in Your Dreams
As your Greatest Fantasy
Consuming Your Thoughts with Mine
Creating a Connection that's Pure Ecstasy

Will you Let Me See the Passion That I know Resides
I Can Feel It when You Touch Me
Each and Every time You Cum Deep Inside

Finding Comfort in Your Words
While Laying in Your Arms
I Feel at Peace, a Calm Serenity
Safe from all Harm

Can I Touch Your World
And Share Your Space
Kiss Your Mind, Your Inner Soul
Then Leave You Wanting and Needing Me
With Only the Memory of My Face

Journal Entry VII
February 1999

Today was a very good day. Who is this Beautiful Blackman that Captured my heart by simply walking into my office? He reminds me so much of my father.
Kweku Toure even his name is powerful.

Wanting and Needing

Wanting you as my Future

Needing them to let me live beyond my Past....

Wanting You to stand beside Me

Needing them to stand behind me....

Wanting you to open up and let me In

Needing them to open the door and let me Leave....

Wanting you to share More

Needing them to share less....

Wanting you to occupy a place in my Heart

Needing them to share that space

So that we can have a New Start

Wanting and Needing You in My Life

Let Him Go

When love fades and hate is all you know
Look deep within
And let him go

When the laughter is replaced with dreams
That is shattered and sadness fills your heart
Letting him go
Is where you start

When the passion and fire disappears
And the memories of it all
Only causes you tears
Let him go

When your love of you is compromised
And to love him
Means your Demise
Let him go

When Love and respect is no longer shown
And finding comfort
In his arms is gone
Let him go

When joy and peace are felt no more
And rage and fear
Are knocking at your door
Let him go

When silent prayers are replaced with a cry for help
And all you think about are
The secrets that are kept

When love fades and hate is all you know
Look deep within
And Let him go

Where did the Love Go

Sunny Days have turned to Stormy Nights

Where did the Love Go?

Down pour of Darkness causing Poverty, Hate, and Disease
Love is Lost, If only we could See

Where did the Love Go?

No Children playing, No Laughter, Only Fear
Our Parks and Playgrounds are Empty
Children standing on Corners and sitting on Benches
With Broken hearts and eyes filled with Tears.

Sunny Days have turned to Stormy Nights
Where did the Love Go?

Shelter for the Rich, but none for the Poor
Houses are Empty and the Streets are full
Homelessness and Hopelessness
Surrounds us Once More
Love is Lost, If Only we could See

Where did the Love Go?

Visions of Life and Love, Blurred by
Visions of Death and Hate
No Compassion or Compromise
Power of Knowledge replaced with Ignorance and Denial
In Time will cause our Demise

Sunny Days have turned to Stormy Nights
Where did the Love Go?

Look Deep Within

Journal Entry VIII
February 2006

Today I realized just how strong the love I had for my ex was. Today I felt his pain and I haven't spoke of the love we shared for years. God give me the strength to hold this man up when his whole world just clasped around him. How can he go on when he just lost his mother and sister in the same day?

Remembering A King

I woke up this Morning with
Remembrance and Gratitude in my Heart
Fighting back Tears of Joy and Sorrow
For the man who gave us Knowledge and the Power to see a new
Start

I Remembered Dr. King
And all that he gave
His Fight and Struggle for Civil Rights
And all the Changes that he has made

I Remembered his Dreams and Visions of Freedom
And all the Possibilities that could be
As I looked at myself in the mirror I prayed that someday a Child
Would see his Struggle through Me

"Giving Honor to a Great Man"
Dr. Martin Luther King Jr.

Peace and Love
Sharon

Is my Black still Cool

Does the way I wear my hair or the clothes I wear,
Represent me....Or who I'm trying to be.
Is My Black Still Cool?

When I speak are the words spoken out
Of Love and Respect...Or are they Spoken with
Hate and much Regret
Is My Black Still Cool?

When I raise my Fist, Does it Represent Anger
Or does it still mean I have the Power.
Is My Black Still Cool?

Are the visions I have reflective of the
Hopes and Dreams of my Past...Or are they
Only visions of making Fast Cash
Is My Black Still Cool?

When I Sing, Do the words Lift You Up
Or Do they Bring You Down?
Is My Black Still Cool?

Is My Strength still seen when I stand alone
Or is real Strength shown with a
Million Men standing with me
Is My Black Still Cool?

For My Brothers

World of Silent Pain

I looked into my Soul Today
Looked myself in the eye and saw someone Unrecognizable

The Woman who once smiled, now wore a frown as her Crown
She was Lost, and waiting to be found

The Laughter of her Voice, Was replaced by Screams
Of Love's that no longer existed, who had taken bits and pieces of her Dreams

Of the Woman she was, and no longer would be
She cried as she prayed on Bended Knee

The Tears she cries are no longer for Joy
They are Tears of Pain and Sorrows
Of Lessons Learned, That have replaced her Tomorrows

She no longer Dreams in Color
Only in Black and White, With Memories of Old Lovers and Promises that never came
She is Lost in a World of Silent Pain

Journal Entry IX
February 2008

New Job and a New Chapter of my life begins. Who would have ever thought I would be working for Sony Electronics. Me the "Cautious Simplifier" who only buys what fits into my life, Day 1 and the Challenge Begins.

Positive and Negatives

Positive Life seeking
A negative Wife
Meeting and Pleasing
A different woman every night

Looking and searching for a
Love that will last
He's destroying lives as he fights
To hide the Demons of his past

Not knowing love
Makes him unaware
When he looks at her
And can't feel the love they share

Giving all her love and affection
Meant sometimes forgetting
To Love him required protection

Now the love is fading away
As he takes bits and Pieces
Of her dreams everyday

She remembers Love
And the price
She was willing to pay

She is now a Negative wife
Living a Positive life
Waiting patiently
As it slips away

HIV/AIDS Awareness is Priceless
Protect Life
Protect Love
Protect You

I Cry

When I see the world through a child's eye
Seeing Homelessness and Hopelessness
And no one cares enough to explain why
Alone in my Solitude
I Cry

When I see the woman who is a afraid to Love
Hiding her pain and fears
As she prays to the man above
Asking for a sign and pleading for understanding as to why
Alone in my Solitude
I Cry

For the girl who finds pleasure in his arms
Naive to his status and blinded by his charm
Giving of herself all that she has to give
Now a Positive Life she must live

Seeing no Love or Hope as she looks into his eyes
Alone in my Solitude
I Cry

When I close my eyes and begin to sleep
In my Dreams I realize
That Child...That Woman and That Girl Is Me

Still seeking answers to my questions
And needing to know why
Alone in my Solitude
I Still Cry

"Making a Difference is Giving your Time
Mentoring a Child....Empowering a Life"

Sharon Johnston

Journal Entry
June 2, 2010

Today I celebrate "Me" and day 46 of this Journey called "Life." I have been Blessed with Family, Friends, and People who have surrounded me that have been a part of each experience and the years that have molded me into the woman I am today. I would not trade any of my years or the people who have shared them. Thank you all for loving me a supporting me through my Journey.

Your Smile

Yours is a smile that steels the qualities of the sun and poor them into a glass for my libation

I am thirsty no longer yet my hunger last long after the last drop of your smile is swallowed and the glass of you is empty or so it seems

Until the next smile appears and tomorrow starts today a new and my thirst returns and we start over again in the moment that you steal the qualities of the Sun and piss off the rest of the world living in darkness but me.

I am a glow, Radiant Yours is the moment in life that defines how foolish men spend their lives counting the breathes they take...... While I want to spend my life counting how you take my breath way!!!

For yours is the smile that steals the radiance of the sun and pours it into a glass and allows me to fill my soul long after your glass is empty and then we simply start again...

Dedicated to Yours Truly by Patrick McDonald

I See Perfection

I see Perfection in you the way the sun rises to the east and sets in the west

I see Perfection in your eyes and the way your smile calls my name without uttering a word

I see Perfection even in the way your body trembles as I approach with my own gaze

I see Perfection in the stars that are flung across heavens sky

I see Perfection How I wish you had seen mine. We could have drank from each others Challis as though we were timed and aged wine....to Perfection of course

I see Perfection even as you search to see it in you

I see Perfection in all that we don't do. Your hands, your hair, your eyes, your kisses missed and promised to yesterdays and tomorrows with today's envy just the same.

I see Perfection when your smile simply mentions without words, the utterance of my name.

The Perfection you seek is there and is so clear to me...

Ode to Sharon
By Patrick McDonald

Eternal Peace Within A Souls Journey: My Life My Love My Poetry
Copyright © 2011 by Sharon Johnston

All rights reserved. No part of this book may be reproduced in any form or by any electronic or mechanical means including storage and retrieval systems without permission in writing from Sharon Johnston

Acknowledgements
Cover and Author Photos by: Smile Collector Photography
Dedicated Poems "Your Smile and "I See Perfection" by Patrick Mc Donald

Printed in the United States of America
Self Published by Sharon Johnston